S0-BID-764

# Graham Greene

## by FRANCIS WYNDHAM

Published for the British Council
and the National Book League
by Longmans, Green & Co

*Three shillings and sixpence net*

Graham Greene is among the leading English novelists writing today. Introducing this survey of his work, Francis Wyndham suggests that Greene's development has revealed an attempt to restore 'religious sense and the sense of the importance of the human act to the English novel'. A convert to Catholicism, he is obsessed by the themes of fear, love and despair and man's search for salvation, and these themes are fully developed in his best novels, notably *The Power and the Glory* and *The Heart of the Matter*. All his writing, which includes a number of successful plays, many short stories and critical articles and some film scripts, is marked by an outstanding technical skill, which has increased over the years.

Mr Wyndham, who has been reviewing books for British newspapers and journals for twenty years, examines the qualities that have contributed to Greene's widespread recognition abroad as well as in his own country. This study of the whole range of his writing will be welcomed by general readers as well as students of contemporary literature.

*Bibliographical Series*
*of Supplements to* 'British Book News'
*on Writers and Their Work*

GENERAL EDITOR
Geoffrey Bullough

Karsh

GRAHAM   GREENE

# GRAHAM GREENE

by

## FRANCIS WYNDHAM

PUBLISHED FOR
THE BRITISH COUNCIL
AND THE NATIONAL BOOK LEAGUE
BY LONGMANS, GREEN & CO

LONGMANS, GREEN & CO LTD
Longman House, Burnt Mill, Harlow, Essex

*Associated companies, branches and*
*representatives throughout the world*

*First published 1955*
*Revised 1958, 1962, 1966, 1968*
© Francis Wyndham 1958, 1962, 1966, 1968

*Printed in Great Britain by*
*F. Mildner & Sons, London, EC1*

# GRAHAM GREENE

## I

'WITH the death of James, the religious sense was lost to the English novel, and with the religious sense went the sense of the importance of the human act.' Graham Greene, an English novelist considered by many to be among the most gifted now writing, says this while speaking of François Mauriac; he goes on to add that Mauriac's 'first importance to an English reader, therefore, is that he belongs to the company of the great traditional novelists: he is a writer for whom the visible world has not ceased to exist, whose characters have the solidity and importance of men with souls to save or lose, and a writer who claims the traditional and essential right of a novelist, to comment, to express his views'. The words are significant: Greene's own development as a novelist has revealed above all an attempt to restore these two qualities—religious sense and the sense of the importance of the human act—to the English novel; to give back to it that extra dimension which places characters against the background of a world in which they are seen through the eyes of God. However unimportant they may seem in the world of the senses—for he often chooses to portray the weak, the failures—they have an overwhelming importance in another world. Indeed, perhaps through their very weakness and sense of failure they have an especial love for God which makes them the 'heroes' of Greene's books: 'it is the love for God that mainly survives because in his eyes they can imagine themselves always drab, seedy, unsuccessful, and therefore worthy of notice'. Greene's preoccupation with the seedy and the sordid—'seediness has a very deep appeal', he writes in *Journey Without Maps*—springs from this: 'it seems to satisfy, temporarily, the sense of nostalgia for something lost; it seems to represent a stage further back'.

5

'In all writers there occurs a moment of crystallization when the dominant theme is plainly expressed, when the private universe becomes visible even to the least sensitive reader.' The words are Greene's. The dominant theme was stated, tentatively, in his first novel, and appeared again and again throughout his work, becoming crystallized with his acceptance—he was not converted, he says, since his was an intellectual conviction and not an emotional one—of the Roman Catholic faith. This was the turning-point in his career: from then on the conflict between good and evil that takes place daily within a man's soul tended to become more and more specialized within the terms of Greene's own faith.

One is struck, when reading the earlier books, by the invariable presence of the element of pursuit: the pursuit of a criminal by the police, a traitor by those whom he has betrayed, a victim by his persecutors. It symbolized the pursuit of man's soul, his inner self, by God; he was hunted down in his search for a peace that often was found only in death. Later, the religious theme became more explicit: God was the pursuer from whom there could be no escape, even when despair dictated a way out that looked, from the Catholic point of view, like damnation. Caught between pain and pain, tormented by pity, afraid of damnation, Greene's characters are often the victims only of their own unforgettable love for God.

Yet with all this, his development as a novelist has not entirely pleased either his fellow Catholics or his non-Catholic readers. For many Catholics he has sailed too near the wind of the things that lead to damnation: he has exposed 'all the beauty and the horror of the flesh'. In *Brighton Rock*, his first specifically Catholic novel, he was on safe ground: the conflict between good and evil, damnation and salvation, was clearly defined. But in his later novels there was a mingling of good and evil, strength and weakness in his central characters; moreover his concern with adultery and physical love has disturbed some of his Catholic critics. On the other hand, to non-Catholics his sense of sin has been distasteful; his preoccupation with evil and with squalor has seemed over-emphatic, almost gloating; much of the suffering he emphasizes has appeared pointless and artistically unjustified. The struggle that he analyses in his later book between salvation and damnation is often unnecessarily tortuous; the final miracles explicitly treated of in *The End of the Affair*, and hinted at in earlier novels, have been regarded as stretching things too far.

The answer is that Greene's view-point and the working-out of his themes demanded just such conclusions. He had to carry to their absolute ends both what he believes to be the human capacity for love, pity, fear and, above all, despair, and God's capacity for mercy. Whether such conclusions are always technically and artistically successful is a different matter.

Violence again characterizes many of his novels. These are 'thrillers', with murder, suicide and betrayal as their ingredients. He has, too, a feeling for cruelty which is only made bearable by his compassion. Partly the violence of which he writes is symbolical of the struggles going on all the time within men's souls; partly it is the expression of the brutality and violence of our world. 'Today our world seems peculiarly susceptible to brutality. There is a touch of nostalgia in the pleasure we take in gangster novels, in characters who have so agreeably simplified their emotions that they have begun living again at a level below the cerebral . . . when one sees to what unhappiness, to what peril of extinction centuries of cerebration have brought us, one sometimes has a curiosity to discover if one can from what we have come, to recall at which point we went astray.'

*The Man Within*, Greene's first novel, was published in 1929. Here the theme of pursuit is expressed in clear-cut terms: 'A sense of overwhelming desolation swept over him, a wonder whether he would ever know peace from pursuit. . . .' The hero, if hero he can be called, has betrayed his fellow smugglers to the excisemen; he takes refuge from his avengers in a girl's house and she persuades him to give evidence in court against his accomplices. The pursuit is both actual and symbolic: in the words of Sir Thomas Browne: 'There's another man within me that's angry with me.' Andrews is a coward; he has some groping sense of peace in his love for the girl, seeing in her a love for God which he does not possess. In her death he is able to find himself, to identify himself with that 'stern unresting critic' which was the 'man within'.

The same tradition of historical adventure story is followed in two other books—*The Name of Action* and *Rumour at Nightfall*—both of which were afterwards suppressed by the author. None of the three can be called a distinguished novel—they are oddly obscure, and the characters are pasteboard—but it can be said that in them Greene was stating the themes that he was afterwards to work out with success.

Perhaps they are insufficiently integrated because all this time Greene was working as a journalist. This is evident in some of his traits of style: tricks of observation—a half-eaten sausage-roll in a saucer, the cigarette ash on the trousers—little crudities and sensationalisms, an occasional over-pithiness. They are faults that have tended to fall away from him over the years, but they are still detectable here and there.

## II

Greene's reputation was established by his fourth novel, *Stamboul Train*. He called it 'an entertainment'—a name which he has given to seven of his books by way of distinguishing them from his more serious works. It was written in a hurry, he said later, 'because one desperately wanted the money'. This fact is perhaps evident in the book, which lacks cohesion, but both as a thriller and as a foretaste of what he can do in the way of characterization, it is excellent.

*It's a Battlefield* is a bitter and ironic novel which mirrored a good deal of political unrest in the country when it was published in 1934. A Communist bus-driver has wounded a policeman during a political riot because he thought that the policeman was going to strike his wife; the policeman has died and the bus-driver has been sentenced to death for murder. At the time that the book opens his appeal has failed and it remains to be seen whether the Home Secretary will grant him a reprieve. The title of the book is taken from Kinglake's *Eothen*.

In so far as the battlefield presented itself to the bare eyesight of men, it had no entirety, no length, no breadth, no depth, no size, no shape, and was made up of nothing except small numberless circlets commensurate with such ranges of vision as the mist might allow at each spot. . . . In such conditions, each separate gathering of English soldiery went on fighting its own little battle in happy and advantageous ignorance of the general state of the action; nay, even very often in ignorance that any great conflict was raging.

There is a deadly irony about the little battles that are being fought here, while all the time one is conscious of the 'general state of the action' behind them: the newly appointed Commissioner of Police afraid of retirement and loneliness, preoccupied with the Paddington murder and the Streatham Common rape, eyed with suspicion by his subordinates, hounded by the bus-driver's brother who longs to do something to justify his manhood and who sleeps with his brother's wife as much out of pity as lust; the pathetic journalist; the idealistic Frenchman; the reprieve which depends for its granting on the political situation. The final irony comes when it is granted, for the bus-driver's brother has died of shock after an accident believing that he has failed, and the prison chaplain has resigned as a protest against the horror of keeping a young man in prison for eighteen years. The pity of it is that in this book Greene has been defeated by his own ends: like *Stamboul Train* it is too diffuse; too many characters spoil the total impact.

The novel which followed, *England Made Me*, is possibly Greene's most ambitious book; it is not, however, his most successful because in it he has aimed at something which he has only imperfectly achieved. For the first and last time in his work he uses the stream-of-consciousness technique. Artistically the book is a failure: it, also, is too diffuse; moreover, somewhere he loses control of his raw material and the final effect is one of dissatisfaction. Nevertheless, in feeling the book is deeper than anything he had written hitherto, and the bitterness and irony here have a subtler edge; for all its imperfections, it has great interest for his admirers.

At this time, Greene made a journey through the Republic of Liberia, through areas where in living memory no white man had seen, where no proper maps were available, and where tropical diseases were rampant. It was a strange and often terrifying journey: one feels that his reasons for making it were something like those that sent the hero of *The Name of Action* on an unconsidered adventure to Trier: 'his only hope of escape from a life of which he had grown inexpressibly tired, a life without meaning, without risk and without beauty.' At any rate, in the forests of Africa he discovered in himself a passionate interest in living. 'I had always assumed before, as a matter of course, that death was desirable', he writes in *Journey Without Maps*, the book which was the fruit of his 350-mile journey. Like 'the revolver in the corner cupboard' with which as a boy he played a game of chance, and about which he writes in an essay in *The Lost Childhood*, Africa was an escape from the intolerable burden of ennui.

Thus, *Journey Without Maps* is interesting chiefly for its subject-matter and for the vivid descriptions that Greene gives of people and places. But it is interesting, too, for what it tells one about its author: the way in which Africa seemed familiar to him, like something to which one gropes back under psychoanalysis; the fascination that the seediness of the civilization of the coast exercised over his mind, the sense of disappointment when the journey was finished and he could go back to civilization as we know it. Later, during the war he was to return to the British colony of Sierra

Leone for the Foreign Office, where he found the raw material for his best book, *The Heart of the Matter*.

Diverging now to 'entertainment', as he called it, he next gave his readers *A Gun for Sale*; although in bare content a thriller, this contains a psychological study as arresting as any that he presents in his novels.

'Murder didn't mean much to Raven. It was just a new job.' Raven has been hired as an assassin by a firm of armament manufacturers to kill the head of a European state; he is to be paid two hundred pounds for his work and as far as he is concerned that will be the end of the matter: the repercussions do not interest him. But the two hundred pounds is reported to the police as stolen money and Raven is on the run, while in Europe war is threatening. His path is crossed by a girl, the actress with whom the police inspector in charge of the case is in love; Raven intends to make use of her and then to kill her. But because of her compassion—as he sees it—she is spared, and for the first time in his life he gives someone his trust, in telling her everything. For her his story means the avoidance of war: she believes him and sticks by him in order to prove it, but in the end she is driven to betray him, as he has always been betrayed. For Raven has a hare-lip, 'like a badge of class. It revealed the poverty of parents who couldn't afford a surgeon'. All his life he had been conscious of his own ugliness, of the repulsion that he inspired in others; this, and the father hanged in Wandsworth prison and the mother with her throat cut had conditioned his life.

Raven foreshadows Pinkie, the boy gangster in *Brighton Rock*, but whereas Pinkie, being a Catholic, is fully aware of the nature of his own wickedness, Raven is amoral: he regards the whole structure of religion as so much claptrap, associating it with all that he had been taught in the institution in which he was brought up:

In a religious shop by the Catholic Cathedral he found himself facing again the images that angered him in the Soho café: the plaster mother and child, the wise men and the shepherds. They were arranged in a cavern of brown paper among the books of devotion, the little pious scraps of St Theresa. 'The Holy Family': he pressed his face against the glass with a kind of horrified anger that tale still went on. 'Because there was no room for them in the inn': he remembered how they sat in rows on the benches waiting for Christmas dinner, while the thin precise voice read on about Caesar Augustus and how everyone went up to his own city to be taxed. Nobody was beaten on Christmas Day: all punishments were saved for Boxing Day. Love, Charity, Patience, Humility: he was educated: he knew about those virtues; he'd seen what they were worth. They twisted everything: even that story in there, it was historical, it had happened, but they twisted it to their own purposes. They made him a God because they could feel fine about it all, they didn't have to consider themselves responsible for the raw deal they'd given him. He'd consented, hadn't he? That was the argument, because he could have called down 'a legion of angels' if he'd wanted to escape hanging there. On your life he could, he thought with bitter lack of faith, just as easily as his own father taking the drop at Wandsworth could have saved himself when the trap opened. He stood there with his face against the glass waiting for somebody to deny that reasoning, staring at the swaddled child with a horrified tenderness, 'the little bastard', because he was educated and knew what the child was in for, the damned Jews and the double-crossing Judas and only one man to draw a knife on his side when the soldiers came for him in the garden.

But in death his bitterness is somehow transformed:

the only problem when you were once born was to get out of life more neatly and expeditiously than you had entered it. For the first time the idea of his mother's suicide came to him without bitterness, as he fixed his aim at the long reluctant last and Saunders shot him in the back through the opening door. Death came to him in the form of unbearable pain. It was as if he had to deliver this pain as a woman delivers a child, and he sobbed and moaned in the effort. At last it came out of him and he followed his only child into the darkness.

There is much compassion in *A Gun For Sale*: compassion which makes the reader feel tenderness and sympathy for Raven. But there is irony and bitterness, too, in the terrible picture it presents of society: the Midland manufacturing town; the armaments king who says that a murderer ought not to be allowed to benefit from his crime while calmly planning to start a war through the death of a boyhood friend; the seedy, half-comic, half-tragic life backstage of the local repertory theatre, in the straggling rows of decaying houses, in the local medical school.

## III

The first positive indication of Greene's conversion to the Roman Catholic faith was *Brighton Rock*, published in 1938. Hitherto, the conflict within his characters had been a general one: from now on it tends to become increasingly specialized. Pinkie, the boy gangster, with his 'face of starved intensity', is a Catholic. So, too, is Rose, the girl he marries in order to prevent her from going to the police. Pinkie is wicked, but he is aware of his own wickedness, half in love with the idea of Hell: at the back of his mind is the thought of repentance, 'of making peace, of going home, and his heart weakened with a faint nostalgia for the tiny dark confessional box, the priest's voice, and the people waiting under the statue, before the bright lights burning down in the pink glasses, to be made safe from eternal pain'. Later damnation came to him as something he could accept: 'He had a sense that he would never be scared again: running down from the track he had been afraid, afraid of pain and more afraid of damnation—of the sudden and unshriven death. Now it was as if he was damned already and there was nothing more to fear ever again.'

Like Raven, Pinkie has been conditioned by his upbringing. His horror of sex as an act of darkness springs from the tiny room in which on every Saturday night he had watched from his single bed his parents performing the 'exercise'. On one of the few occasions when he is articulate for any length of time he describes the death of a young girl on the railway line, her head severed: she was going to have her second baby; when her first was born any of a dozen youths might have been its father.

Rose is good, and she, too, knows the nature of her sin when she marries Pinkie in a registry office. But she will risk damnation for him, out of love and a blind trust in the mercy of God. Ida Arnold, who suspects Pinkie and works to convict him of murder, is the good pagan:

No real sense of danger could lodge behind those large vivacious eyes. Nothing could ever make her believe that one day she too would be where the worms . . . her mind couldn't take that track; she could go only a short way before the switch automatically shifted and set her vibrating down the accustomed line, the season-ticket line marked by desirable residences and advertisements for cruises and small fenced boskages for rural love.

There is an intense pathos about Fred Hale, Pinkie's victim, with his fears and his weak heart and varicose veins and bad liver; about Spicer, the man who gets scared after the murder and is conveniently killed by a falling bannister; above all, about Rose, who could bear anything so long as she thought Pinkie loved her, but for whom the full horror of realization was to come.

*Brighton Rock* made a successful film, because it has a film technique in much of its writing. But it is repetitive, often, in its ideas: Pinkie's horror of sex, for instance, is overdone. Also, there is a certain priggishness, a certain Catholic partisanship, which detracts from its worth.

In the spring of 1938 Greene was commissioned to visit part of Mexico in order to write a book about the religious situation at a time of persecution. *The Lawless Roads* is, therefore, not an ordinary travel book, but specifically a book about religion, and despite the charm of many of his personal descriptions—of American travellers, old settlers, Germans, Indians—it is chiefly for his attitude to the religious problem that the book is interesting. Also, it was on this journey that he found the material for his very fine novel, *The Power and the Glory*.

The Church in many parts of Mexico had been persecuted and religious services forbidden, but everywhere people continued to honour the God that they were not allowed publicly to worship. As a Catholic, Greene's attitude was not unnaturally clear:

> I went into the Templo del Carmen, as the dark dropped, for benediction. To a stranger like myself it was like going home—a language I could understand—'*Ora pro nobis*'. The Virgin sat on an extraordinary silver cloud like a cabbage with the Infant in her arms above the altar; all along the walls horrifying statues with musty purple robes stood in glass coffins; and yet it was home. One knew what was going on. Old men came plodding in in dungarees and bare feet, tired out with work, and again I thought: how could one grudge them the gaudy splendour of the giltwork, the incense, the distant immaculate figure upon the cloud? The candles were lit, and suddenly little electric lights sprayed out all round the Virgin's head. Even if it were all untrue and there was no God, surely life was happier with the enormously supernatural promise than with the petty social fulfilment, the tiny pension and the machine-made furniture.

The way in which the poor squeezed the last drop of mortification out of their already terribly hard lives convinced Greene of the vital need these people felt for their religion: for the gilt and incense and ceremony. He hated Mexico, but at times it seemed as if there were worse places. 'Here were idolatry and oppression, starvation and casual violence, but you lived under the shadow of religion—of God or the Devil.' On the other side there was nothing— 'just the drugstore and the Coca-Cola, the hamburger, the graceless sinless empty chromium world'.

*The Power and the Glory* was Greene's best novel to date when it was published in 1940, being at once more concentrated and economical in its effects than anything he had written previously. For the first time he had succeeded completely in relating his characters and story to form a coherent, taut whole.

It is set in the primitive landscapes of the Mexico of *The Lawless Roads* (reading the two books one can find many parallels in the writing), during a time of political strife and religious persecution in the nineteen-twenties. All the

priests have fled or been shot or have made their submission
to authority by marrying. (There is a brilliant study of old
Padre José, who has married a great mountain of flesh in the
form of a nagging wife.) One priest has eluded capture and
is being harried by his pursuers throughout the state with a
price on his head. He is a bad priest—'a whisky priest'—
with a child of his own whom he cannot help but love. He
longs for the peace of confession, but here he is, condemned
to go round making 'God knew what martyrs' when he
feels that he himself is 'without grace enough to die'.

When the book opens, he is about to escape, but he gives
up the chance in order to visit a woman who is reputed to be
sick. He is a priest and there is nothing he can do except go
on. The English child who gives him shelter asks him why
he does not renounce his faith:

'He said: "It's impossible. There's no way. I'm a priest. It's out of my
power." '
'The child listened intently. She said: "Like a birthmark." '

Again he is about to escape when he is called to the death-
bed of an American gangster. He knows that it is a trick,
that he will be betrayed by the half-caste who has followed
him, waiting for just such an occasion, but he cannot refuse
to go. It is his duty to give the man absolution. The irony is
that the gangster refuses to make his confession: his last
thought before he dies is for the priest's safety. But he is
taken and shot. As Greene wrote of his actual counterpart,
in *The Lawless Roads*: 'He was little loss, poor man, but who
can judge what terror and hardship and isolation have
excused him in the eyes of God?' At any rate, in a charac-
teristic final scene he suggests that the whisky priest's prayer:
'Oh, God, send them someone more worthwhile to suffer
for'—had been answered. A boy who has witnessed the
death of the priest before the firing squad has gone to bed
when he hears an insistent knocking at the door. Wearily,
he gets up, knowing that his father is out and that it is his
duty to answer the knocking:

Slowly he made his way across the patio towards the outer door. Suppose it was the lieutenant come back to revenge himself for the spittle. . . . He unlocked the heavy iron door and swung it open. A stranger stood in the street: a tall pale man thin with a rather sour mouth, who carried a small suitcase. He named the boy's mother and asked if this were the señora's house. Yes, the boy said, but she was asleep. He began to shut the door, but a pointed shoe got in the way.

The stranger said: 'I have only just landed. I came up the river tonight. I thought perhaps . . . I have an introduction for the señora from a great friend of hers.'

'She is asleep,' the boy repeated.

'If you would let me come in,' the man said with an odd frightened smile, and suddenly lowering his face he said to the boy: 'I am a priest.'

'You?' the boy exclaimed.

'Yes,' he said gently. 'My name is Father—.' But the boy had already swung the door open and put his lips to his hand before the other could give himself a name.

*The Power and the Glory* is a considerable advance on *Brighton Rock* because in it good and evil, weakness and strength, are more truly mingled in the central character of the priest than they are in the separate characters of Pinkie and Rose. The rest of the characterization, too, is brilliant: Mrs Fellowes, the Englishwoman to whom even to speak of life is to remind her with terror of death; the young-old child, her daughter; Mr Tench, the seedy English dentist with his stomach pains; the half-caste who betrays the priest.

Shortly before the publication of *The Power and the Glory*, Greene published a grim little 'entertainment', *The Confidential Agent*. It is not up to the standard of his other entertainments: written on the eve of war, it is a thriller with pursuit, fear and desperation as its ingredients, but with the underlying horror of the ruthlessness of war in which human life is expendable.

Another entertainment followed *The Power and the Glory*, set in wartime London, *The Ministry of Fear*. This, too, is a secret service thriller, but with, as in *A Gun for Sale*, a psychological import. The chief character is a man pursued by pity and terror. He has a few years before killed his wife out of pity for her, dying slowly in agony from a long illness. He has been tried for murder, but acquitted, and since then has longed to receive in some way the punishment that he has felt to be his due. Accidentally he is involved with a ring of enemy agents and has to flee from a murder which he has not committed: a murder staged to frighten him. In a bomb explosion he loses his memory: its gradual return and his dawning realization that he is a murderer are beautifully treated, though the process by which he finds salvation is a little obscure.

## IV

Compassion runs as a strong thread through all Greene's work: in *The Heart of the Matter* he carries the character of Rowe in *The Ministry of Fear* to its terrifying logical conclusion. Scobie in *The Heart of the Matter* is truly three-dimensional in a way that no other character had been in Greene's work to date. He is a Catholic, converted when he married his pious Catholic wife. As Deputy Commissioner of Police in a West African district he is above all a just man, incorruptible: this, perhaps, is the reason why he is passed over for promotion. A man so treated is expected to retire, but retirement to him is worse than death (an echo of the Commissioner of Police in *It's a Battlefield*): 'the thought of retirement set his nerves twitching and straining: he always prayed that death would come first'. But it is his wife whose feelings are most outraged by the news of his failure, and it is the pity which he feels for her as she lies under her mosquito-net like 'a joint of meat under a meat-cover'—even that image is quickly hustled away by pity—that sets in train a course of events which is to lead to disaster. Louise wants to get away to South Africa for a holiday: she hates the society in which she is condemned to live, knowing that everyone laughs at her. Scobie promises her that she shall go, although he knows that he has not got the money for her passage:

No man could guarantee love for ever, but he had sworn fourteen years ago, at Ealing, silently during the horrible little elegant ceremony among the lace and candles, that he would at least always see to it that she was happy. . . . He would still have made the promise even if he could have foreseen all that would come of it. He had always been prepared to accept the responsibility for his actions, and he had always been half aware too, from the time he made his terrible private vow that she would be happy, how far *this* action might carry him. Despair is the price one pays for setting oneself an impossible aim. It is, one is told, the unforgivable sin, but it is a sin the corrupt or evil man never practises. He always has hope. He never reaches the freezing-point of knowing absolute failure. Only the man of goodwill carries always in his heart this capacity for damnation.

This, as far as Scobie goes, is the heart of the matter. He is a good man, but his fatal weakness is that he cannot bear to hurt those whom he loves. Pity for Louise, a passion more intense than love, drives him to borrow money from a Syrian trader in order to send her to South Africa. While she is away he falls in love with a nineteen-year-old widow who is brought to the colony as a survivor from a torpedoed ship. Here again, it is pity from which his love springs: pity for this child hovering between life and death, still clutching the stamp album that her father gave her on her fourteenth birthday. Scobie's own child had died, but he had been spared witnessing her death: what follows is in a way an expiation for the guilt that he has secretly felt for this. Out of pity as much as love (another echo of *It's a Battlefield*) he begins an affair with Helen Rolt and an indiscretion involves him further and further with the Syrian: the incorruptible man sees himself caught up in corruption. Unexpectedly Louise, who has heard about the affair which Scobie imagines he is so well concealing, returns. She asks him to go with her to Holy Communion, well knowing that he cannot do so in a state of mortal sin. Scobie cannot hurt her by refusing, but at the same time he cannot hurt Helen by giving her up, and he is too honest to promise in confession to do something that he knows he cannot. In this matter the priest fails to help him, and with the knowledge of damnation in his heart he receives Communion. (There is a wonderful description of his feelings as he approaches the Sacrament.)

Caught between pity and pity, and knowing that he cannot continue to wound God—'striking God when he's down'—he methodically plans his suicide in such a way that neither Louise nor Helen will know that he took his own life.

*The Heart of the Matter* can be called a study in despair, despair as the Roman Catholic Church knows it, but it does not end there. There is Scobie's last cry: 'Dear God I, love . . .'; there is the last chapter when Louise, who has had it suggested to her by the special agent from London who is in love with her, realizes that Scobie killed himself and goes to see the priest:

'He was a bad Catholic'.

'That is the silliest phrase in common use,' Father Rank said.

'And at the end this—horror. He must have known that he was damning himself.'

'Yes, he knew that all right. He had never had any trust in mercy—except for other people.'

'Its no good even praying . . .'

Father Rank clapped the cover of the diary to and said, furiously, 'For goodness' sake, Mrs Scobie, don't imagine you—or I—know a thing about God's mercy.'

'The Church says . . .'

'I know the Church says. The Church knows all the rules. But it doesn't know what goes on in a single human heart.'

'You think there's some hope then?' she wearily asked.

'Are you so bitter aginst him?'

'I haven't any bitterness left.'

'And do you think God's likely to be more bitter than a woman?' he said with harsh insistance, but she winced away from the arguments of hope.

'Oh, why, why did he have to make such a mess of things?'

Father Rank said, 'It may seem an odd thing to say—when a man's as wrong as he was—but I think, from what I saw of him, that he really loved God.'

She had denied just now that she felt any bitterness, but a little more of it drained out now like tears from exhausted ducts. 'He certainly loved no one else,' she said.

'And you may be in the right of it there, too,' Father Rank replied.

*The Heart of the Matter* is Greene's best book because of its tautness, economy and evenness of style. Only here and there is a jarring note struck: Scobie's imaginings about his daughter, had she lived, for instance:

> He thought: If my child had lived, she too would have been conscriptable, flung into some grim dormitory, to find her own way. After the Atlantic, the A.T.S. or the W.A.A.F., the blustering sergeant with the big bust, the cook-house and the potato peelings, the Lesbian officer, with the thin lips and the tidy gold hair, and the men waiting on the Common outside the camp, among the gorse bushes . . .

The effect of the heat is beautifully done, although here again he tends to use the same image more than once, which immediately weakens its power, as it did in *Brighton Rock*: here, it is the blotting paper put under the wrist while writing to absorb the sweat. The characterization is excellent, not only in the case of Scobie, but also in that of Helen, Louise, the priest conscious of his inadequacy, the pathetic Harris, the brash Wilson.

But it is also Greene's best book because in it he has fully and finally developed the themes that have run through all his novels: the pity, fear, love and despair; the search of a man for salvation. He has, too, carried to its conclusion the implications of his own faith—the love and mercy and mystery of God.

After *The Heart of the Matter*, *The End of the Affair* reads like a disappointing postscript. It is written mainly in the first person of a middle-aged novelist who has an affair with the wife of a civil servant: two years before the book opens she has ended their relationship without ever giving him a reason. Casually meeting her husband, the 'I' of the book sets out on a diabolical quest to find out what his ex-mistress is doing, in the course of which he stumbles on the truth in her diary. She has given him up because she had believed him dead in an air-raid and had prayed for a miracle: if he was returned to life she had vowed to leave him. The diary, which forms part of the novel, is something of a *tour de force*: it describes her painful awareness of God, her struggle to escape from Him, to find a reason to break her vow. When her lover discovers that she still cares for him, he goes to her house to persuade her to return. But she is ill, and the next thing he hears is that she is dead. Although he learns that she had wanted to become a Catholic, he persuades her husband to have her cremated: later he discovers that as a child she had been baptized into the Catholic Church. There follows what can only be described as a series of miracles.

Despite the brilliance of the diary, *The End of the Affair* is an artistic failure. The first person technique makes for a lack of detachment that prevents the reader from ever seeing the story in perspective. At times it is embarrassingly personal. The time sequences, moving from past to present, are unnecessarily hard to follow. The miracles, even if they are perfectly logical in the terms of Greene's faith, fail to be an organic part of the book and simply strike a false note, as though they have been tacked on. It is for these reasons that the book must be regarded as a stumble in Greene's progress.

Greene's first work for the theatre, *The Living Room*, is a further development of the themes of despair and the problem of the Catholic in relation to an impossible physical love. It is, too, a terrible indictment of the pious Catholic, just as the character of Louise Scobie was, though for her one could feel pity. Rose is the daughter of a Catholic mother and a non-Catholic father who begins an affair with a middle-aged psychiatrist who is her trustee, on the night after her mother's funeral. She comes to stay with her two great-aunts and her great-uncle, a crippled priest, whose failure to provide the right words of comfort at the right time has much in common with Father Rank's. The conflict which develops for Rose when she finds herself caught between the pain of giving up her lover and the pain of hurting his wife leads in the end to a despair akin to Scobie's and she takes her own life, a childish prayer on her lips.

The significance of the title of the play is contained in the fact that the two old women are so afraid of death that they will not use any room in which someone has died—so that they are now left with a bedroom, next to a lavatory, as a living-room. In this room Rose dies, and it is a mark of God's forgiveness that her death so reassures and comforts the elder of the two women that, so far from not wishing to sleep in the room in which she died, she voluntarily chooses to do so: 'There'd be no better room for me to fall asleep in for ever than the room where Rose died.'

The failure of both priest and psychiatrist leaves room only for the mercy of God; but whereas in *The Heart of the Matter* Greene succeeds in conveying the meaning and purpose of Scobie's action, in the case of *The Living Room* one is left with a sense of waste.

## V

A short novel which appeared in 1955, *Loser Takes All*, amply justified its designation of 'entertainment'; written with a professional ease that approaches slickness, it is highly diverting but makes no claim to be considered among Greene's important books.

This was soon followed by *The Quiet American*, a full-length novel which used the war in Indo-China as a background. The war scenes in this book contain some of Greene's most brilliantly successful descriptive writing, and were the fruit of first-hand observation. As the story is not this time directly concerned with the subtleties of the Roman Catholic conscience, it was suggested that he had temporarily abandoned religious themes; but careful readers will recognize in it the same complex moral problems, the pity and the anger to be found in most of his later work. It is a version of the theme, beloved by Henry James, of American optimism and innocence at sea in an old world of violence and corruption, treated with a bitterness that is unmistakably Greene's own. Fowler, the narrator, says of the quiet American, Pyle: 'I never knew a man who had better motives for all the trouble he caused', summarizing the story of the book; and also, summarizing the theme, 'You can't blame the innocent. . . . All you can do is to control them or eliminate them. Innocence is a kind of insanity'. Fowler sees to it that the well-meaning, slow-thinking, high-minded Pyle is eliminated before he can cause yet more damage; but his own motives are suspect to himself, for Pyle has taken his mistress from him. Yet the guilty, decadent Fowler is presented as more sympathetic a character than the blundering, but 'good' and earnest Pyle. A possible criticism of this book is that the important figure of the American is rather flatly conceived—is, in fact, a caricature; but the neat complexity of the story, and the fine descriptive passages, give it an important place among Greene's serious fiction.

In his second play, *The Potting Shed*, he returns to a subject within a specifically Roman Catholic context. The technique with its taut construction, atmosphere of mystery, abundance of 'clues' in the early scenes and emphasis on suspense, resembles that of a thriller. Indeed, the play could be described as a spiritual detective story. A respected agnostic, Grand Old Man of liberal humanism, is dying off-stage—how bitterly the author mocks his dedicated but misguided life! His family and his best friend are nervous and guilty about some secret event that took place years ago, something to do with the potting shed in the garden and his younger son James. It eventually emerges that what they are trying to conceal was nothing less than a miracle, performed by the dying man's despised brother, a priest, who sacrificed his faith to save his nephew's life.

*The Complaisant Lover*, Greene's third play, is lighter in tone: in fact it contains one scene that recalls a Feydeau farce.

Yet it has under-currents of sadness. It is about a middle-aged dentist, his wife, and his wife's lover. As the title suggests, the husband condones his wife's infidelity, but this is not through indifference or cynicism. He loves her with an understanding love that is no longer possessive; he wants her happiness more than his own. Both *The Potting Shed* and *The Complaisant Lover* were successful on the stage, but they are far from being Greene's best work: the first is contrived and melodramatic, the second superficial and sentimental. With his seventh 'entertainment', however, the short novel called *Our Man in Havana*, Greene returned to his best form. The irony here is finer than in *Loser takes All*, and the technical skill as unobtrusively consummate.

Three years later, in 1961, he published *A Burnt-Out Case*. An elaborately plotted spiritual melodrama, executed with the economy of a master, it contains a great deal (perhaps too much) that is typically Greene. Marie Rycker, for instance, the child-woman, with her touchingly *bourgeoise* tastes and her prattle about her convent school, is a figure that the author himself has turned into a cliché. The same is true of the seedy journalist. 'There is a strong allurement in corruption and there was no doubt of Parkinson's: he carried it on the surface of his skin like phosphorus, impossible to mistake.' Here the writer gives the effect of imitating —even parodying—himself. The background, a leper Colony in the Belgian Congo, is established with all his wizardry at evoking atmosphere; and yet we feel, irrationally, that we have been here before. It is with slight surprise that we realize that this is the first of his novels to be set in such a place; we have recognized, not the atmosphere of the *léproserie*, but the climate of Graham Greene's world.

Yet there is something new in *A Burnt-Out Case*. This is the character of Querry, whose predicament is referred to by the title. A successful man who has come to the end of success, he is the victim of a terrible attack of indifference. Greene quotes from Dante: 'I did not die, yet nothing of life remained.' A sensualist for whom pleasure has gone stale, an artist for whom art has lost its meaning, he is a tragic and arresting creation. The rest of the book—the background, the plot, the other characters, the conversations— seem artificially constructed to frame his portrait.

Later in the same year, Greene published an interesting pendant to this novel: *In Search of a Character*, which consists of two African Journals. The shorter covers a voyage from Liverpool to Freetown in 1941; the more important journal was written in the Congo, when he was gathering the material for *A Burnt-Out Case*. This provides a fascinating glimpse, as it were, into Greene's workshop, and also confirms a suspicion that the central character of the novel— the burnt-out case—may have been more autobiographical in conception than is usual with Graham Greene's heroes.

Any fears that Greene's own talent was burning itself out were completely allayed by his next publication. Consisting of one short novel and three longish stories, *A Sense of Reality* is among the most satisfactory of his achievements. *A Discovery in the Woods* is a macabre exercise in post-nuclear prophecy and *Under the Garden* successfully alternates between reality and a dream. In these tales Greene for the first time experiments with fantasy; but he does so in a manner entirely his own.

Realism is even further abandoned in the play *Carving a Statue*, which was a failure when performed in 1964: a rare occurrence for Greene. The central character is a sculptor obsessed by his work on a gigantic statue of God the Father. As in *The Complaisant Lover*, Greene's treatment explores the relationship between tragedy and farce. The result proved too static for the theatre, but it contains some fine imaginative passages which can be better appreciated when read.

The theme of indifference, adumbrated in *A Burnt-Out Case*, is treated with greater elaboration and complexity in *The Comedians*, a substantial novel published in 1966. Violence can be the expression of love, indifference never. One is an imperfection of charity, the other the perfection of egoism.' Greene has already shown us that pity (*The Heart of the Matter*) and innocence (*The Quiet American*) can be dangerous, leading to violence, their apparent opposite. Now he seems to suggest that playing safe is the most dangerous course of all—that anything, spiritually speaking, is better than nothing. His comedians are the indifferent, the egoists, the uncommitted, who play life as a charade, exploiting it or enduring it as a background to their own half-hearted attempts at survival. They experience sex without love, enthusiasm without faith, adventure without conviction. A preface warns against autobiographical indentification: 'I want to make it clear that the narrator of this tale, though his name is Brown, is not Greene.' (Other leading characters are called, not quite facetiously, Jones and Smith.) In form the novel is a return to the fictional-reportage manner of *The Quiet American*: this time, it is the corrupt Negro republic of Haiti that is brilliantly illuminated by the author's superb journalistic sense. This talent for vivid description of a landscape, a culture, an atmosphere, a complex society, is again slightly at odds with the more strictly imaginative aspects of the novel: the artificial plot, like some elaborate dance of death, and the symbolic properties of the characters who move through it. As a narrative, *The Comedians* is one of Greene's most exciting and varied performances, a *tour de force* astonishing in its scope and assurance. It only lacks the purity—the apparently inevitable harmony between theme and drama, content and style—of his very best work.

It is interesting that this most recent of Graham Greene's novels echoes a theme found in *The Man Within*, his first: the subleties of treachery. Brown betrays Jones because of a groundless sexual jealousy. Betrayed, the disreputable Jones accidently translates his lies into reality; this comedian becomes, in death, almost a tragic figure. But not quite: 'for what truth did Jones die?' As for the contemplative and cynical Brown, we leave him in Santo Domingo, doing well in the undertaking business. 'I had felt myself not merely incapable of love—many are incapable of that, but even of guilt. There were no heights and no abysses in my world—I saw myself on a great plain, walking and walking on the interminable flats.'

The remainder of Greene's writings consists of a number of short stories, articles and essays; work for the films, and some stories for children. The earlier stories are sidelines to his work as a novelist, as in *The Third Man*, well known as a film, which was never written to be read, but only to be seen. 'The Basement Room', the story from which the film, *The Fallen Idol*, was made, is interesting in its use of a technique that he also used tentatively with one character in *A Gun for Sale*—a sort of God's-eye view into the future. The small boy in 'The Basement Room' is to witness something that he will carry with him until the day he dies. 'He would never forget that scene. In a week he had forgotten it, but it conditioned his career, the long austerity of his life.' 'The End of the Party' is a grim little story which uses the idea of the peculiar relationship existing between twins that was also used in *England Made Me*. A recent collection called *May We Borrow Your Husband?* is accurately sub-titled 'and other comedies of the sexual life'. Polished, ironic, mildly outrageous, there tales are skilful exercises in the anecdotal *genre* of Maupassant and Maugham, with a hint of despair underlying the sophistication that is typical of Greene. The essays and articles have been published in a volume called *The Lost Childhood*: his critical work is fresh and stimulating, and throws much light on his own work as a novelist.

Fear, pity, violence, pursuit and the endless, restless quality of man's search for salvation and of God's love for man, are the recurring themes of Greene's novels. These have been interpreted with outstanding technical ability; everything he writes is readable. Acute observation, a style which maintains, without obscurity, a high level of intensity, a sensitivity to atmosphere (especially to certain seedy aspects of modern life which he was among the first to capture in print, so that his readers often say of a character or a place, 'Just like something in Graham Greene!'): these are among his assets. Some find his continual emphasis on squalor and seediness, his slightly adolescent *nostalgie de la boue*, his almost ridiculous addiction to describing such subjects as lavatories, indigestion and the less appealing side of sexual adventure, an irritating drawback to enjoyment of his work. Certainly these are overdone; possibly they give his books a spurious attraction to some readers: however, his sincerity is never in question. It will be interesting to see how in the future he will further develop his remarkable gifts; and it is a sign of his originality and versatility that no easy prediction of the course he will follow has ever been possible.

# GRAHAM GREENE

## A Select Bibliography

(Place of publication London, unless stated otherwise)

*Collected Works:*

UNIFORM EDITION, 15 vols (1947—)
—Volumes published to date: 1. The Man Within; 2. Stamboul Train; 3. It's a Battlefield; 4. England Made Me; 5. Journey Without Maps; 6. A Gun for Sale; 7. Brighton Rock; 8. The Confidential Agent; 9. The Power and the Glory; 10. Ministry of Fear; 11. The Heart of the Matter; 12. Twenty-One Stories; 13. The End of the Affair; 14. The Lawless Roads; 15. The Quiet American.

*Separate Works:*

BABBLING APRIL; Oxford (1925). *Verse*

THE MAN WITHIN (1929). *Novel*

THE NAME OF ACTION (1930) *Novel*
—the author has directed that this and the following novel should not be reprinted.

RUMOUR AT NIGHTFALL (1931). *Novel*

STAMBOUL TRAIN (1932). *Entertainment*

IT'S A BATTLEFIELD (1934). *Novel*

THE OLD SCHOOL, ed. Graham Greene (1934)
—contains an introduction and essay.

THE BASEMENT ROOM (1935). *Stories*
—reprinted with nine additions as *Nineteen Stories*, 1947. Seventeen of the *Nineteen Stories*, with an additional four stories (published for the first time in book form) appear as *Twenty-One Stories* in the Uniform Editions.

THE BEAR FELL FREE (1935) *Short Story*
—limited edition of 285 copies, 250 for sale, signed by the author.

ENGLAND MADE ME (1935). *Novel*

JOURNEY WITHOUT MAPS (1936). *Travel*

A GUN FOR SALE (1936). *Entertainment*

BRIGHTON ROCK (1938) *Novel*
—the American edition, 1938, was classified as *Entertainment.*

THE LAWLESS ROADS (1939). *Travel*

THE CONFIDENTIAL AGENT (1939). *Entertainment*

THE POWER AND THE GLORY (1940). *Novel*

THE MINISTRY OF FEAR (1943). *Entertainment*

NINETEEN STORIES (1947). *Stories*

THE HEART OF THE MATTER (1948). *Novel*

WHY DO I WRITE? (1948). *Letters*
—an exchange of letters between Elizabeth Bowen, Graham Greene and V. S. Pritchett.

THE THIRD MAN and THE FALLEN IDOL (1950). *Entertainments*

THE LITTLE FIRE ENGINE (1950). *Pictorial Juvenile*
—in collaboration with the illustrator, Miss D. Craigie.

THE LOST CHILDHOOD AND OTHER ESSAYS (1951). *Essays*

THE END OF THE AFFAIR (1951). *Novel*

THE LITTLE HORSE BUS (1952). *Pictorial Juvenile*
—in collaboration with the illustrator, Miss D. Craigie.

THE LIVING ROOM (1953). *Drama*

THE LITTLE STEAMROLLER (1953). *Pictorial Juvenile*
—in collaboration with the illustrator, Miss D. Craigie.

TWENTY-ONE STORIES (1954). *Stories*

LOSER TAKES ALL (1955). *Entertainment*

THE QUIET AMERICAN (1955). *Novel*

THE POTTING SHED, New York (1957). *Drama*

THE SPIES BEDSIDE BOOK, ed. Graham Greene and Hugh Greene. (1957)
—contains an Introduction.

OUR MAN IN HAVANA (1958). *Entertainment*

THE COMPLAISANT LOVER (1959). *Play.*

A VISIT TO MORIN (1959)
—limited edition 250 copies.

A BURNT-OUT CASE (1961). *Novel*

IN SEARCH OF A CHARACTER (1961). *Two African Journals*

AFRICAN SKETCHBOOK, by F. Francks (1962)
—contains a preface by Graham Greene.

THE BODLEY HEAD FORD MADDOX FORD (1962)
—contains an introduction by Graham Greene.

A SENSE OF REALITY (1963). *Four Stories*

CARVING A STATUE (1964). *Play*

THE COMEDIANS (1966). *Novel*

MAY WE BORROW YOUR HUSBAND? (1967). *Stories*

*Note:* *Novel* and *Entertainment* are the author's terms for differentiating his serious and light fiction.

*Some Critical Studies:*

GRAHAM GREENE, by J. Madaule, Paris (1949).

GRAHAM GREENE TÉMOIN DES TEMPS TRAGIQUES, by P. Rostenne; Paris (1949).

THE ART OF GRAHAM GREENE, by K. Allott and M. Farris (1951).

GRAHAM GREENE AND THE HEART OF THE MATTER, by M.-B. Mesnet (1954)
—mainly concerned with the three 'Catholic' novels, *Brighton Rock*, *The Power and the Glory* and *The Heart of the Matter*.

GRAHAM GREENE, by J. Atkins (1957).

GRAHAM GREENE: SOME CRITICAL CONSIDERATIONS, ed. R. O. Evans; Kentucky (1963)
—contains a good bibliography.

GRAHAM GREENE, by D. Pryce-Jones; Edinburgh (1963).

GRAHAM GREENE, by D. Lodge; New York (1966).

Acknowledgements are gratefully made to William Heinemann Ltd for permission to quote the extracts from *A Gun for Sale*, *Brighton Rock*, *The Power and the Glory* and *The Heart of the Matter*.

# WRITERS AND THEIR WORK

*General Editor:* GEOFFREY BULLOUGH

*The first 55 issues in the Series appeared under the General Editorship of* T. O. BEACHCROFT
*Issues 56-169 appeared under the General Editorship of* BONAMY DOBRÉE

*General Surveys:*

THE DETECTIVE STORY IN BRITAIN:
Julian Symons
THE ENGLISH BIBLE: Donald Coggan
ENGLISH VERSE EPIGRAM:
G. Rostrevor Hamilton
ENGLISH HYMNS: A. Pollard
ENGLISH MARITIME WRITING:
Hakluyt to Cook: Oliver Warner
THE ENGLISH SHORT STORY I: & II:
T. O. Beachcroft
THE ENGLISH SONNET: P. Cruttwell
ENGLISH SERMONS: Arthur Pollard
ENGLISH TRAVELLERS IN THE
NEAR EAST: Robin Fedden
THREE WOMEN DIARISTS: M. Willy

*Sixteenth Century and Earlier:*

FRANCIS BACON: J. Max Patrick
BEAUMONT & FLETCHER: Ian Fletcher
CHAUCER: Nevill Coghill
RICHARD HOOKER: A. Pollard
THOMAS KYD: Philip Edwards
LANGLAND: Nevill Coghill
MALORY: M. C. Bradbrook
MARLOWE: Philip Henderson
SIR THOMAS MORE: E. E. Reynolds
RALEGH: Agnes Latham
SIDNEY: Kenneth Muir
SKELTON: Peter Green
SPENSER: Rosemary Freeman
THREE 14TH-CENTURY ENGLISH
MYSTICS: Phyllis Hodgson
TWO SCOTS CHAUCERIANS:
H. Harvey Wood
WYATT: Sergio Baldi

*Seventeenth Century:*

SIR THOMAS BROWNE: Peter Green
BUNYAN: Henri Talon
CAVALIER POETS: Robin Skelton
CONGREVE: Bonamy Dobrée
DONNE: F. Kermode
DRYDEN: Bonamy Dobrée
ENGLISH DIARISTS:
Evelyn and Pepys: M. Willy
FARQUHAR: A. J. Farmer
JOHN FORD: Clifford Leech
GEORGE HERBERT: T. S. Eliot
HERRICK: John Press
HOBBES: T. E. Jessop
BEN JONSON: J. B. Bamborough
LOCKE: Maurice Cranston
ANDREW MARVELL: John Press
MILTON: E. M. W. Tillyard

RESTORATION COURT POETS:
V. de S. Pinto
SHAKESPEARE: C. J. Sisson
CHRONICLES: Clifford Leech
EARLY COMEDIES: Derek Traversi
LATER COMEDIES: G. K. Hunter
FINAL PLAYS: F. Kermode
HISTORIES: L. C. Knights
POEMS: F. T. Prince
PROBLEM PLAYS: Peter Ure
ROMAN PLAYS: T. J. B. Spencer
GREAT TRAGEDIES: Kenneth Muir
THREE METAPHYSICAL POETS:
Margaret Willy
IZAAK WALTON: Margaret Bottrall
WEBSTER: Ian Scott-Kilvert
WYCHERLEY: P. F. Vernon

*Eighteenth Century:*

BERKELEY: T. E. Jessop
BLAKE: Kathleen Raine
BOSWELL: P. A. W. Collins
BURKE: T. E. Utley
BURNS: David Daiches
WM. COLLINS: Oswald Doughty
COWPER: N. Nicholson
CRABBE: R. L. Brett
DEFOE: J. R. Sutherland
FIELDING: John Butt
GAY: Oliver Warner
GIBBON: C. V. Wedgwood
GOLDSMITH: A. Norman Jeffares
GRAY: R. W. Ketton-Cremer
HUME: Montgomery Belgion
JOHNSON: S. C. Roberts
POPE: Ian Jack
RICHARDSON: R. F. Brissenden
SHERIDAN: W. A. Darlington
CHRISTOPHER SMART: G. Grigson
SMOLLETT: Laurence Brander
STEELE, ADDISON: A. R. Humphreys
STERNE: D. W. Jefferson
SWIFT: J. Middleton Murry
SIR JOHN VANBRUGH: Bernard Harris
HORACE WALPOLE: Hugh Honour

*Nineteenth Century:*

MATTHEW ARNOLD: Kenneth Allott
JANE AUSTEN: S. Townsend Warner
BAGEHOT: N. St John-Stevas
THE BRONTË SISTERS: P. Bentley
BROWNING: John Bryson
E. B. BROWNING: Alethea Hayter
SAMUEL BUTLER: G. D. H. Cole